DATE DUE

Great African Americans

Carter G. Woodson

the father of Black History

Revised Edition

Patricia and Fredrick McKissack

Series Consultant
Dr. Russell L. Adams, Chairman
Department of Afro-American Studies, Howard University

Enslow Publishers, Inc.

40 Industrial Road   PO Box 38
Box 398   Aldershot
Berkeley Heights, NJ 07922   Hants GU12 6BP
USA   UK

http://www.enslow.com

To Barbara, T.J., and C.C.

Revised edition of *Carter G. Woodson: The Father of Black History* © 1991

Library of Congress Cataloging-in-Publication Data

McKissack, Pat, 1944–
    Carter G. Woodson : the father of Black history / Patricia and Fredrick McKissack.— Rev. Ed.
      p. cm. — (Great African Americans)
    Includes Index.
    ISBN 0-7660-1698-6
    1. Woodson, Carter Godwin, 1875–1950—Juvenile literature. 2. Afro-American historians—Biography—
Juvenile literature. 3. Historians—United States—Biography—Juvenile literature. 4. Afro-Americans—
Historiography—Juvenile literature. [1. Woodson, Carter Godwin, 1875–1950. 2. Educators. 3. Historians.
4. Afro-Americans—Biography.] I. McKissack, Fredrick. II. Title.
    E175.5.W65 M35   2001
    973'.0496073'0092—dc21

                                      00-012417

Printed in the United States of America

10 9 8 7 6 5 4 3 2

Illustration Credits: The Association for the Study of African-American Life and History, Inc., p. 25; Library of Congress, pp. 6 (inset), 7, 10, 15, 16, 18, 19, 21B, 23T, 23B, 24; Moorland-Spingarn Research Center, Howard University, pp. 3, 4, 12; National Archives, p. 20, 27; Private collection, p. 21T; The Rare Book, Manuscript and Special Collections Library, Duke University, pp. 6, 8; U.S. Postal Service, p. 26; West Virginia State Archives, p. 11.

Cover Illustration: Library of Congress; Moorland-Spingarn Research Center, Howard University; National Archives.

table of contents

CARTER G. WOODSON
December 19, 1875–April 3, 1950

CHAPTER 1

Family Stories

The first history lessons Carter Woodson learned were about his own family. His mother, Anne Eliza Riddle, was born a slave. She told stories about her life.

Carter's father told him stories, too. James Henry Woodson was also born a slave. His master beat him all the time.

One day James took the whip away from his master and beat him with it. A group of men came

5

As slaves, Carter's parents had to work in the tobacco fields.
The leaves were picked by hand, then hung to dry.

to kill James. But he ran and hid in the woods for many, many days.

It was near the end of the Civil War. Soldiers from the North were in Virginia. They found James in the woods. They told him he was free. James joined the Union Army.

Carter's father was a scout for the Union Army. He gathered information for the northern soldiers in the Civil War.

Carter was born on a farm in Virginia.

The war ended in April 1865. Soon after, James and Anne met and married. They moved to Huntington, West Virginia.

In 1874 they moved back to New Canton, Virginia. They bought a small farm. Carter was born there on December 19, 1875.

CHAPTER 2

Never Too Late to Learn

Carter's father couldn't read or write. But he always told his seven children, "It is never too late to learn."

Carter had to help out on the family farm. There wasn't much time for school. Still he learned how to read. He read every day.

When Carter was sixteen years old, he went to West Virginia with his older brothers. There he worked on the railroad and in a coal mine.

9

By 1893, Anne and James had moved back to Huntington, West Virginia. Carter had two younger sisters. They wanted to go to Douglass High School. Carter wanted to go there, too.

But he was eighteen years old. "It is never too late to learn," he told the principal.

Carter had learned a lot on his own. He did very well on a test. So they let Carter start at Douglass High School. Then he surprised everyone when he graduated eighteen months later.

Next Carter went to college. After a few months, he was asked to be the principal of a school.

Like these men, Carter worked hard in the coal mines.

10

Carter and his sisters went to high school in Huntington, West Virginia.

He had that job for two years. In the summers, he went to school.

In 1900, Carter was asked to be the principal of Douglass High School back in Huntington. He was proud to take the job. He stayed there three years.

Carter read every day. He tried to learn something new every day. He read to his students. And he always told them, "It is never too late to learn."

"It is never
too late
to learn."
Carter
was a
very good
teacher,
too.

CHAPTER 3

"Shake the Lomboy Tree"

On August 31, 1903, a letter came for Carter. He had been asked to come teach in the Philippine Islands. His work began on December 19, 1903.

Something was wrong. The children weren't learning. They didn't like to read. The other teachers said the children were lazy. Or their mothers and fathers didn't care. Carter wouldn't stop trying.

One day he sang a song for his students: "Come Shake the Apple Tree." But apples don't grow in the Philippines! So Carter changed the words to "Come Shake the Lomboy Tree." A lomboy is a kind of plum. The children loved the song. They wanted to learn it. And they did.

Carter learned Spanish. He taught the children about their own history and heroes. The children were proud of who they were. Soon they were reading and learning quickly.

Singing a song about a fruit tree made learning fun.

After that, Carter put away the books. They were written for American children.

14

**Carter taught English to students in the Philippines.
The grass hut was their school building.**

Carter wanted history books to teach about African Americans, too.

Carter thought about the school books back home. They didn't have much black history in them. Carter wrote home. "It is time to 'Come Shake the Lomboy Tree' in American schools."

16

CHAPTER 4

Teach Ourselves

each summer Carter came home. He studied history at the University of Chicago. He came home for good in 1908. He needed to learn more. So he went to the University of Chicago. He graduated in March. He continued his studies and earned a higher degree in August of that same year.

Then Woodson went to Harvard University in

Woodson studied history at the University of Chicago.

Massachusetts. There he worked on the highest degree a student can earn—a Ph.D. He received his Ph.D. in history in 1912. With that degree, he was called Dr. Woodson.

Dr. Woodson took a job at M Street High School in Washington, D.C. There he taught history, French, and Spanish.

Woodson earned a Ph.D. in history from Harvard University.

History books still didn't have much about black people in them.

19

Dr. Woodson never married. When friends asked why, he said, "It wasn't because I didn't ask."

"We must teach ourselves," he said. At Dr. Woodson's school, black history was taught.

In 1914, Dr. Woodson became a member of the American Negro Academy. The group found and saved African-American writings. They wanted to show that black people had done many important things in history.

Dr. Woodson started the Association for the Study of Negro Life and History in 1915. "We will teach ourselves about ourselves," he said.

Dr. Woodson wrote many books. He also started this magazine about African-American history.

THE JOURNAL
OF
NEGRO HISTORY

CARTER G. WOODSON
EDITOR

VOLUME I

1916

THE ASSOCIATION FOR THE STUDY OF NEGRO LIFE
AND HISTORY, Inc.
LANCASTER, PA., AND WASHINGTON, D. C.
1916

W. E. B. Du Bois, right, said education was very important. Dr. Woodson agreed.

CHAPTER 5

Be Proud

most schoolchildren didn't know about the important things black people had done. Dr. Woodson wrote about these great African Americans.

Dr. Woodson had an idea that would help people learn more about black history.

Two of Dr. Woodson's heroes were Frederick Douglass and Abraham Lincoln. Douglass fought against slavery. And President Lincoln freed the slaves. Both men were born in February.

**Frederick Douglass, left, and Abraham Lincoln
were two of Dr. Woodson's heroes.**

"Be proud!" Because of Dr. Woodson, students learned about their African past.

In February 1926, Dr. Woodson planned the first "Negro History Week" program. It was the start of what is now called Black History Month.

Dr. Woodson studied and wrote about Africa,

THIRTY-FIRST ANNUAL CELEBRATION OF
NEGRO HISTORY WEEK
FEBRUARY 12-19, 1956

THE ASSOCIATION FOR THE STUDY OF NEGRO LIFE AND HISTORY
1538 NINTH STREET, Northwest, WASHINGTON 1, D. C.
Founded by Carter G. Woodson (1875-1950)

Since the 1920s, black history programs like this one have been held all over the country.

25

This 1984 postage stamp honors Carter G. Woodson.

too. He wanted black people to know about their African ancestors. "Africa has a great past," he told schoolchildren all over the country. "Be proud!"

Dr. Woodson stopped teaching to run the association full-time. He never married. He lived over the association's office in a small apartment. He was a neat man who liked nice clothes. He was always busy, but he was hardly ever late.

On April 3, 1950, Dr. Woodson was late for work. Something had to be wrong. And it was. He had died during the night.

Dr. Woodson's work helped show the world that African Americans had much to be proud of. Today his work goes on.

Dr. Woodson was proud of African Americans.
He devoted his life to learning
and teaching the story of his people.

timeline

1875 ~ Carter Godwin Woodson is born in Virginia.

1895 ~ Enters high school in Huntington, West Virginia.

1897 ~ Enters Berea College in Kentucky.

1903 ~ After finishing college, teaches in the Philippine Islands

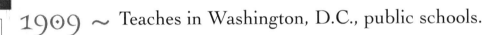

1903

1908 ~ Earns master's degree from the University of Chicago; enters Harvard University.

1909 ~ Teaches in Washington, D.C., public schools.

1912

1912 ~ Receives Ph.D. in history from Harvard.

1915 ~ Founds the Association for the Study of Negro Life and History; publishes the first of many books on African-American history.

1926 ~ Begins Negro History Week (which later becomes African History Month); receives Spingarn Medal from the NAACP.

1933 —1939 ~ Publishes several more books on African-American history.

1950 ~ Dies on April 3 in Washington, D.C.

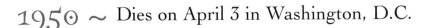

WORDS TO KNOW

Africa—The second largest continent in the world.

American Negro Academy—An organization that found and saved African-American writings.

ancestors—People who lived long ago, and are related by family or race.

Association for the Study of Negro Life and History—An organization started to teach black people about themselves and their history.

Civil War—A war fought within one country. The United States Civil War was fought between northern and southern states from 1861 to 1865.

coal mine—A mine is a place in the ground where minerals like coal, gold, and silver are dug out.

college—A school beyond high school.

degree—A signed piece of paper that a college or university gives a person when he or she has graduated.

graduate—To finish all the studies at a school.

hero—A person who is looked up to because of the things he or she does.

WORDS TO KNOW

lomboy tree—A plum tree that grows in the Philippine Islands.

master—A ruler or a person who controls another. Someone who owns a slave is called a master.

National Association for the Advancement of Colored People (NAACP)—An organization started to help all Americans gain equal rights and protection under the law. The NAACP is one of the oldest civil rights organizations in the United States.

Ph.D.—The highest degree a student can earn from a university. It means doctor of philosophy.

Philippine Islands—A group of small islands in the South Pacific Ocean.

principal—The head of a school.

slave—A person who is owned by another. That person can be bought or sold.

Union Army—The army that fought for the North in the Civil War.

Washington, D.C.—The place where the United States government is located. (D.C. stands for District of Columbia.)

Learn more about Carter G. Woodson

Books

Haskins, Jim. *Carter G. Woodson: The Man Who Put "Black" in American History*. Brookfield, Conn.: Millbrook Press, 2000.

Goggin, Jacqueline. "Carter Godwin Woodson," in Jack Salzman, David Lionel Smith, and Cornell West, eds., *Encyclopedia of African American Culture and History*. New York, N.Y.: Simon & Schuster, 1996.

Read about African-American history

Hoobler, Dorothy and Thomas. *The African American Family Album*. New York, N.Y.: Oxford University Press, 1995.

Johnston, Brenda A. *Stories from Black History*. Cleveland, Ohio: New Day Press, 1993.

Internet Addresses

Black History: Virginia Profiles
   <http://www.timesdispatch.com/blackhistory/
   MGB28FPSAIC.html>

Ebony magazine article about Dr. Woodson
   <http://usinfo.state.gov/usa/blackhis/woodson.htm>

index